# JOAN CHITTISTER

# the breath
## OF THE soul

### REFLECTIONS
### ON PRAYER

For more information about Joan Chittister, OSB, please visit her Web site: www.benetvision.org

**Second printing 2009**

TWENTY-THIRD PUBLICATIONS
A Division of Bayard
One Montauk Avenue, Suite 200
New London, CT 06320
(860) 437-3012 or (800) 321-0411
www.23rdpublications.com

The Scripture passages contained herein are from the *The Inclusive Bible: The First Egalitarian Translation*, copyright ©2009, by Sheed and Ward. All rights reserved.

ISBN 978-1-58595-747-7
Library of Congress Catalog Card Number: 2009926105

Printed in the U.S.A.

# CONTENTS

# Introduction

This is a small book. More important, it is a very simple book. It does not teach a prayer form. It does not provide prayers for every occasion. It is not a history of prayer styles or theologies. It is neither a primer in prayer nor a discussion of the effects of prayer.

But it does attend to what we are most inclined to forget. It is a discussion of the attitudes that prepare us for prayer. It is an examination of what we ourselves must bring to the discipline of prayer—whatever forms it takes—in order to make prayer an authentic and real, a deep and profound part of our lives.

Prayer is the link to a life beyond the mundane, the daily, the routine, the immediate dimensions of life. It is the beginning of a relationship with the God who is closer to us than we are to ourselves. It is a relationship with both creation and the Creator. It grows us into the fullness of ourselves, both spiritually and psychologically.

But authentic prayer requires something from us, as well as from the God whom we seek. It requires, among other things, that we bring to it an open heart, a good deal of self-knowledge, constancy in darkness and a willingness to attend to the Light, even when all we can see is darkness.

Spiritual elders from every tradition anchor each chapter of the book. Their words carry us through a spiritual history that is tried and true. They set our sights. They give us the fruits of hundreds of years of spiritual search. They become the spiritual mentors of our own generation as they were of generations before us.

Each segment of the book is meant more to be a reflection on their insights than it is a lesson, in the educational sense of the word. It is not meant to be "studied," it is meant to be absorbed. Each segment is simply another way into prayer and designed to be of the process of prayer itself. It asks the question, "How much self-knowledge am I really bringing to my prayer?" for instance. And it requires an answer—week after week, year after year.

None of the segments is ever finished, ever closed, ever fully resolved. They are all ongoing steps along the way, steps we retrace over and over again as we do all the other parts of life, until they become the very breath we breathe, the vision and energy of our souls.

To aid in this deepening process of prayer, every section ends with a short sentence, a mantra, which, said over and over again throughout the day, hammers one particular quality of prayer or another deeper and deeper into our hearts as the days and years go by.

Finally, the Scripture passage at the end of each segment illuminates the process of prayer from the very core of the Scriptures. It embeds us in the teaching and the life of salvation history. It binds us and our prayer life to the very beat of the heart of God.

Read the book in any order that appeals to you as you begin. Read the same chapter as many times as you want before you go on to another one. Allow the mantras themselves to guide your prayer life for a while. Most of all, let the book pour gently into your soul. Don't swallow it whole. Let every segment wash over you again and again. Let each of them become your prayer until, eventually, the words begin to disappear and only the reality of them remains.

# 1. Self-knowledge

*Pray as you can and do not try to pray as you can't. Take yourself as you find yourself; start from that.*

— DOM CHAPMAN

Prayer forms are a good thing to cultivate in the spiritual life. They give structure to our prayer life. A prayer form tells us how to sit when we pray. It tells us what to say and how to say it—or better yet, perhaps, what not to say and how not to sit.

Prayer forms are designed to calm us down when we're too agitated to concentrate. They center us in the midst of the natural distractions and noise of life. In many cases, they even provide the content that a soul that is dry or weary or perturbed simply cannot always provide for itself. They fill the emptiness that sets in when prayer becomes just one more effort I have too little energy to make.

No doubt about it: prayer forms are part of the superstructure of a serious prayer life. But they are not everything. Prayer is about a great deal more than simply the way we pray or even the prayers we pray.

The everything of a deep and demanding prayer life is an awareness and acceptance of the self. No rosary, no icon, no prayer corner can supply for the raw material of prayer, which is the self-knowledge that cements the relationship between the self and God.

The temptation with which we must grapple if we really want to learn to pray is the temptation to pray as if we were more than we are. More pious, perhaps. More accepting of the will of God, maybe. More ethereal in our concerns. More otherworldly, more a citizen of the next world than a pilgrim in this one.

But when all we bring to prayer is our holiness, what is the use of being there? What am I not facing in myself that really needs my prayer if I am ever to grow in the art of prayer and the mandate to become fully human—if I am ever to become more than I am in the spiritual life?

5

To grow spiritually, then, I cannot hide—even from myself. I must pray for self-knowledge, for the searing honesty that, with the grace of God, can bring me to the heart of God.

Self-knowledge saves us from ourselves.

**MANTRA:** *God, be merciful to me a sinner.*

Two people went up to the Temple to pray; one was a Pharisee, the other a tax collector. The Pharisee stood and prayed like this: "I give you thanks, O God, that I'm not like others—greedy, crooked, adulterous—or even like this tax collector. I fast twice a week. I pay tithes on everything I earn." The other one, however, kept a distance, not even daring to look up to heaven. In real humility, all the tax collector said was, "O God, be merciful to me, a sinner."

❧ LUKE 18:10–13

# 2. Responsibility

*Never pray in a room without windows.*

❧ THE TALMUD

The rabbis are clear: Prayer is not meant to make us into a world unto ourselves. We do not pray in order to escape the world around us. We pray with one eye on the world so that we can come to understand what is really being asked of us here and now, at times like this, as co-creators of the universe.

When God put humankind into a garden called earth, it was, Scripture is clear, to steward it to fullness of life. We were intended to keep the earth in good condition, to use it and develop it, to be fruitful and to multiply its creative energies, to do our part in bringing every aspect of creation to fulfillment.

What God did not complete, we are meant to finish. God gave us the plants and intends us to garden and harvest them for the good of the entire world. God gave us the sun and intends us to use its energies in ways that maintain not destroy life. God gave us all the raw materials of life—physical, psychological and mental—and expects us to bring to full growth what was created in embryo.

We must learn to pray with more than ourselves in mind.

We do not pray for our own needs alone. We pray to become holy agents of the God who made us to care for the earth and all its peoples.

We are each workers in the garden of life.

Our most contemplative people—Teresa of Avila, John of the Cross, Catherine of Siena, Ignatius of Loyola, Thomas Merton, Dorothy Day—are those who most actively sought the coming of the reign of God on earth. We pray to become like them.

To be assured that we are living an authentic prayer life we must forever and always examine its fruits in us. Are we really more concerned about others because we have come closer to the God who loves them? Or have we turned prayer into a refuge from what being fully human demands of us?

Prayer is meant to bring us to see the world as God sees the world. It is meant to expand our vision, not trap us in the world that is only ourselves.

Commitment to the needs of the world is a sign of the presence of God in us.

**MANTRA:** *God, give me the grace to "till and keep" the part of the world you have given into my care.*

God blessed them and said, "Bear fruit, increase your numbers, and fill the earth—and be responsible for it! Watch over the fish of the sea, the birds of the air, and all the living things on the earth!"  ❧ GENESIS 1:28

# 3. Enthusiasm for life

*Prayer is our humble answer to the inconceivable surprise of living.*

❧ RABBI ABRAHAM JOSHUA HESCHEL

Some things in life are simply too exciting to ignore. They come when we least expect them. They explode into the middle of the mundane and race through our veins faster than our hearts can handle the pressure of them. They leave us in a kind of spiritual shock, a sort of spiritual numbness.

The conversation we doubted we'd ever have is about to happen. The letter we thought would never come arrives. The opportunity we never dreamed would be offered to us is now, unexpectedly, within reach. Life is suddenly different.

Where do such things come from in the midst of the daily, at the center of unrelenting dullness?

Life simply keeps intruding on our plans, our decisions, our certainties, our fears. What can we say to ourselves about such things?

How can our souls absorb such things, how can our minds make sense of them, how can we possibly respond to them? Most of all, what is their spiritual meaning for us?

Those are not easy questions. They require that we make some decisions about the nature of life itself. As in, is life only random? Does nothing explain the unexplainable? Is there such a thing as destiny? Are we at the mercy of fate? Are we simply pawns in the senseless spinning of an erratic universe?

To live life without living it with exuberance is one of the saddest burdens a person can choose to carry. It is a wound that is self-inflicted. To live with no life in us is a curse of our own making.

As surprising and unsettling as the twists and turns of life may be, it is even more damaging to simply take life itself for granted. If we do that, we are fast on our way to becoming inured to the pulse of life that beats through all our days, however taxing, however difficult. If we miss the little things, we will soon begin to take love and friendship and blessing for granted. Perhaps even miss them entirely. When we do not cultivate a sense of surprise, we give in to the emotional dysfunction that suffocates the breath of life in us. Our hearts go sour and our souls go blind. We lack the open-armed exuberance for life that makes the human human.

It is time to pray for the spiritual consciousness of the unexpected so that Life at work in us can astonish us with its real fullness.

**MANTRA:** *God grant me the gift to live with enthusiasm, to accept life with open, trusting arms.*

Notice how the flowers grow. They neither labor nor weave, yet I tell you, not even Solomon in all his splendor was robed like one of these!

❧ LUKE 12:27

# 4. Discipline

*By a long process of prayerful discipline
I have ceased for over forty years to hate
anybody.*        GANDHI

At no time of day or night are we not thinking about something. The only real question is, What is it? What do I choose to ruminate about in the interstices of the day, in the dark quiet of the night? Where does my mind go when there is nowhere specific defined for it to go?

The question is an important one because its answer defines the kind of person we are choosing to become. If we scheme dark thoughts, however placid and positive we appear to be to others, we are darkness walking. "He was a pleasant man," people say of the felon next to whom they have lived for years. He dressed well, and went to work every day, and nodded to the neighbors. But in his heart the malice simmered and seared.

The fact is that we become what we think about. What we seed in our souls grows in us, forms us, becomes what drives us from moment to moment.

What we think about during the waking hours of the day is basic to prayer. And prayer is also basic to it. What I put into my soul is what will shape me.

Prayer intends to steep me in the thoughts of God, in the sense of the presence of God, in an openness to the will of God, in the likeness of God. To pray is to rivet my mind on the things of God. "As you sweep," our novice mistress taught us, "pray. Just say any short prayer over and over and over," she said. "Eventually it will become part of you." She forgot to say that eventually you will become it, as well.

If, on the other hand, I allow anger to take root in the core of my spirit, let it fester in me, let it bite around the edges of my soul, concentrate on it over and over again—even though the situation that planted it is itself old and musty—whatever the irritation or inconvenience or uncertainty that piques me now, I will become anger, as well.

And, in the same way, I become jealousy. And greed. And lust. And hate. It all depends on what I feed on, what I live on, in my thoughts. What I immerse myself in, down deep inside of me where the soul of a person lies in wait, I will become.

But if I put in the discipline of the presence of God, I will become of God.

If I put in prayer for my enemies, if I pray to a loving God to make me loving, too, then—however many years it takes—it will happen. Then, like a drop of rain in the midst of a flood, I will become part of the heart of the world.

I must pray to become love.

**MANTRA:** *God, free me from my attachment to the evil of hatred.*

Before Jacob died he said to us, "You must say to Joseph: I beg you, please forgive your brothers their crime and their sin and all the wrong they did you. Now, therefore, we ask you, forgive the crime of us who are faithful to the God of your parents." Joseph wept when he heard this…."Don't be afraid; is it for me to put myself in God's place? You planned evil for me, but God planned it for the good….So you need not be afraid."　　　❧ GENESIS 50:17–22

# 5. Constancy

*Late have I loved you, O Beauty, ever ancient, ever new.* ❧ ST. AUGUSTINE

The search for God is the project of a lifetime. It does not come at the instant of an exercise completed. It does not come as an automatic re-action to the keeping of a prayer schedule. More directly, prayer is not the immediate answer to the search for God. Prayer is only the promise that there is purpose to the quest. When we are ready, God will be there. But readiness for God is something to be developed, not something that can be guaranteed.

The Israelites stood far off from Sinai because they knew that to see God face to face could destroy them, burn them to cinders, obliterate them as they had always known themselves to be. And we know that, too.

Instinctively and timidly, we avoid any real encounter with God because we know it will change our lives. Oh, we go through the motions of seeking God, of course. But we find it very hard to believe that God is God: all knowing, all merciful, all loving, all patient.

Because there is no time with God, only eternity, what we did yesterday—a lifetime of yesterdays—is nothing compared with what we finally come to be. Like the workers in the fields who come at the last hour, those of us who spend our lifetimes growing into God will find at the end the very same God that others may come to know long before we do.

Augustine is very clear: Our God does not change. It is we who will change as time goes by. God is God always. And God is with us always. It is we who are so often somewhere else.

After we have sought and gone through all the baubles of life, God is still there waiting for us.

After we have spent our life avoiding God, we find, when we are finally ready and willing to look, that the love of God—still alive in us—still beckons us beyond the frills and fantasies of life to the meaning of what it means to be alive. To the basics of life itself.

It is being wise enough to pray for the grace of awareness of the presence of God that will eventually prepare us to see it in all the dimensions of life. Then we will not treat God as an answer to our problems. We will understand that God is more the Companion whose light shines within us to lead us through them.

There is no such thing as coming too late to God. All the way to God is the Way.

Clearly, we cannot lose God; we can only prepare ourselves to come to see the face of the eternal and ever immediate God in everything. How long will that take? What difference does it make? The God we find when we do will be the same God however long that takes, whenever it happens. It is the journey, not the end, that counts.

**MANTRA:** *Great God, give me strength to persevere in darkness, knowing that you are there in the eternal light I cannot see.*

When those hired late in the afternoon came up, they received a full day's pay, and when the first group appeared they assumed they would get more. Yet they all received the same daily wage. Thereupon they complained to the owner...."My friends," said the owner to those who voiced this complaint, "I do you no injustice. You agreed on the usual wage, didn't you? Take your pay and go home. I intend to give this worker who was hired last the same pay as you. I'm free to do as I please with my money, aren't I? Or are you envious because I am generous?" Thus the last will be first and the first will be last. ❦ MATTHEW 20:9–11, 13–16

# 6. Living in God

*Prayer oneth the soul to God.*

❧ JULIAN OF NORWICH

Prayer, like a laser beam, concentrates the mind and enlarges the soul. It takes us both more into ourselves and out of ourselves at the same time. By calling us to a view of life larger than the present ever can, it deepens the meaning of both the material and the spiritual. It makes them consciously one for us in a world that insists on seeing them as separate. It is in that unity that God exists in us and we in God.

Scientists tell us that matter and spirit are made up of the very same molecules. One is not a different substance than the other. Matter and spirit are, then, the very same thing. The only difference between the two is the density of the molecular structure. The concept of the oneness of the universe is spiritually overwhelming. It gives us an entirely new theological insight into life.

Spirit, then, is not beyond us. On the contrary. Spirit is simply another kind of life. Matter is not non-life, it is simply another level of life. We live in the womb of God, wrapped around by the Spirit of God, energized by the Spirit that is also, at the same time, the same substance that is in matter.

The whole concept enlivens another dimension of life in us, the dimension that does not measure value in terms of higher or lower forms of life. All life is life. All life is permeated by the Spirit of life that is its base. Even at this level of existence there is the reality beyond reality. We live, even here and now, within its arc. We see by its light. We hear its vibrations in everything we do.

But if that is scientifically true it is also spiritually true that prayer is the soul-stretching process that bridges matter and spirit, binds us to the universe, and makes us citizens of the cosmos. It is the outreach of the soul to the Spirit of God in all of creation.

As a result, prayer is clearly the enemy of self-centeredness. It has as its end a relationship with the source of life. It is an entrance to the life that is All Life at once.

Contemporary society demands that we take care of ourselves, that we "advance" and "succeed" and move more and more toward self-sufficiency. The demands of prayer are that we more and more come to understand that it is impossible to be one with God and not be one with the world.

In prayer, then, God's concerns become our concerns. Everything on the globe becomes our business. There is nothing and no one that does not concern us. We simply cannot pray and, at the same time, "mind our own business." Instead, we find ourselves driven to do more and more to make the world what God wants the world to be. "Prayer," as the mystic Julian says, "ones the soul to God."

The Spirit of God comes upon us and, like Jesus, we come to realize that we have come "to do the will of the One who has sent us."

**MANTRA:** *God, give me the insight to understand that to live in the Spirit is to be part of all that is.*

I have given them the glory you gave me that they may be one, as we are one—I in them, you in me—that they may be made perfect in unity.　　　　　　　　　🌿 JOHN 17:22–23

# 7. Prayer and action

*I prayed for twenty years but received no
answer until I prayed with my legs.*

◆ FREDERICK DOUGLASS, ESCAPED SLAVE

P rayer as we know it and talk about it can be very
seductive. "Pray that Grandpa gets well," we
tell a child—all the time knowing that the grandfa-
ther's time is already measured. "Pray for a nice day
tomorrow," we say casually, as if the local meteorol-
ogist doesn't already know whether tomorrow it will
rain or snow. "Dear God, please make Tom call, or
the letter come, or the red light on the next corner
turn green," we recite with a kind of Christian piety
that smacks more of our own desire to run the world
than it does to trust the God who entrusted it to us.

Too often, we use prayer to forgive ourselves for
being less than we are meant to be. "Too often, I'm

praying for it" means that I don't intend to do anything else but pray that someone else will do for us what we should be doing for ourselves.

But the situation is obvious. There is nothing done by humans that humans cannot undo. There is no reason to deny our own responsibility to get it done by foisting it on God. We must get up and do it ourselves.

Or we make prayer a child's game, one step beyond magic or fantasy or folly. When we don't get what we "prayed" for, we break the connection with the Spirit and call the rupture between us a new level of spiritual maturity.

It isn't that God cannot, has not, or will not intervene in nature. There are simply too many things that cannot be explained by nature as we know it to argue for God's indifference to the world. But God does not need to twist the natural law to do it. Once when thunder and lightning came, a more primitive people of another age argued that these things were the voice of an angry god and developed rituals of human sacrifice to appease them. It isn't that thunder and lightning were not real signs of God's presence in the world but, we learned later, not an unnatural one.

The truth is that we must pray for the strength to do what we are meant to do. We must pray for the courage to meet the challenges of life. We must pray for the endurance it will take to go on even when nothing changes. We must pray that the spirit of God is with us as we do what must be done whether we succeed in the process or not.

The ancients talked about four purposes of prayer: adoration, contrition, thanksgiving and supplication. Supplication, what we beg from God, reminds us of our dependence on God. Adoration, contrition and thanksgiving are simply logical extensions of the sense of dependence that reminds us that this God is our beginning and our end—not a magic act in the sky.

**MANTRA:** *God, give me the qualities of character I need to do what you have put me here to do in your name.*

Jesus went on a little further and fell prostrate in prayer: "Abba, if it is possible, let this cup pass me by. But not what I want—what you want."

❧ MATTHEW 26:39

# 8. Humility

*Bow, stubborn knees.*

❧ WILLIAM SHAKESPEARE, *HAMLET*

The greatest obstacle to the spiritual life is the temptation to make ourselves our own God.

It is one thing to know my own gifts and to nurture them. But it is entirely another to presume that I have them all.

The development of our own gifts is the function of giftedness. We have been given natural talents in order to develop them for the sake of others. Each of us has been given something that is meant to make the world a better place for the rest of us. We cook and sing and teach and write and clean and organize in uncommonly common ways. Each of us has something that the rest of the world needs.

We are here to give our gifts to the world, to

wallow in God's gifts to me, yes, but only for the sake of others. We are each only one more link in the chain that is meant to bring all of humanity, everything in creation, to wholeness. What I am and have I must give away recklessly, totally, for the sake of the world. If I don't know my gifts, if I don't develop my gifts I cannot possibly fulfill the purpose of creation in me.

At the same time, it is entirely destructive—most of all, of myself—to presume that because I have one gift that I have all gifts, that no one else has any. That my gift supersedes all others, gives me rights others do not have, authorizes me to live above and beyond the rest of the human race. It is an awful arrogance. It destroys all of our relationships, both human and divine.

Arrogance corrodes our awareness of the power of interdependence and leaves us to die incomplete. It reduces the creation of others to dust. It makes it impossible for us even to see our own needs.

Without the ability to "bow our stubborn knees" to those who are also gifted, we lose the ability even to bow our knee to the Creator who made us each one more beam of Godly beauty which together reflects the radiance that fills the world.

It is our need for one another that teaches us our need for God. It is our down-deep incompleteness that cries out all the days of our lives to be completed—by those around us, by God.

We must pray for the humility it takes to find our wholeness in our littleness.

**MANTRA:** *Great God, give me the humility to see your greatness in others.*

The eye cannot say to the hand, "I do not need you," any more than the head can say to the feet, "I do not need you." And even those members of the body which seem less important are in fact indispensable.

❧ 1 CORINTHIANS 12:21–22

# 9. Authenticity

*The prayer preceding all prayers is, "May it be the real I who speaks. May it be the real Thou that I speak to."*  🐝 C.S. LEWIS

False gods are very easy to come by in life. They seduce us with power and money and fame. They are the things I can't give up, the things I can't do without, the things that shout out my identity to the world so that the world can know how important I am.

We make gods out of the positions we hold. If people don't know what they are, we make sure to tell them.

We make gods out of the social system we have cultivated, about who invites us where to do what.

We make gods out of the money and the baubles and the trinkets of our lives.

We learn even to make gods out of the very religious practices and spiritual disciplines that are meant to lead us beyond ourselves to God. We decide that if we go to church so often, say so many prayers, join so many religious groups, give so much money to the church that we have plumbed the depths of our soul.

And in it all, we develop a totally inauthentic self. Not only do others not know who we really are behind all the bling and titles, but we don't know either. Not only have we fooled others about what we really think and who we really are, too often we fool ourselves as well. More than that, too often we stop thinking about anything of real value at all.

We stop questioning our own motives. We fail to stretch beyond the comfortable spiritual conversations of another time and age. We stop growing inwardly, satisfied with where we have come, however far from the real content of the spiritual life. We play at being spiritual and do not even know we are only playing.

Out of that masking of the self comes another kind of confusion. When we are not bringing an honest self to the search for God we cannot possibly find the real God. We confuse the God of Life with the simpler version—the God of the living. We want God to satisfy our present comforts, not as a guide to growth.

Prayer that emerges out of attitudes of authenticity and honesty, however, takes us beyond all subterfuge, all hiding from God—even behind holy things. It requires us to unmask ourselves to ourselves so that God can come into our lives through the weaknesses, because of which we need God most.

We must learn to pray out of our weaknesses so that God can become our strength.

**MANTRA:** *Dear God, fill me with yourself so that I might be less full of myself.*

God is our refuge and our strength, who from of old has helped us in our distress.

🔖 PSALM 46:1

# 10. Presence

*The fewer the words, the better the prayer.*

O f all the attitudes we bring to prayer, presence is at once one of the simplest and one of the most difficult. Buddhists call it "taming a monkey mind." We call it the need to "resist distractions." Whatever any of us call it, the effects of the condition are the same. We begin to feel far away, even alienated, from the God who seems so far away from us. However much time we put into saying our prayers and going to church, God remains more an idea than a reality. We look for God "to come." We do not expect to find God here.

But where else would God be, if not here? And if here, what creates the Plexiglas between us? "God," Scripture says, "is not in the whirlwind, not in the earthquake, not in the fire." God, Scripture says, "is in the small still voice within." So what is blocking us from making the journey within?

Sinking down into the self where the Spirit resides and the waters run deep is close to impossible in a culture built on noise and talk and information and advertisements and constant movement and a revolving door schedule. Silence and space and solitude are light years away from the raging list of unending activities we carry always in our heads.

Instead, as a culture we are forever on our way to somewhere else. Being here now, bringing to the present moment all the self we have, is more myth than reality. It is an ideal fondly to be acclaimed, seldom to be achieved. People live in buildings full of people now, not even on shady streets with huge yards, let alone on ranches miles apart. We simply do not have much luxury to listen to ourselves anymore, let alone listen to the God within.

Even most of the praying we do is noisy. We say prayers; we seldom simply sit in the presence of God and wait. The very thought of simply listening for the whisper of the soft, still voice within is not only rare, it is uncomfortable these days. Shouldn't we be doing something, our souls shout at us. Shouldn't we be going somewhere, doing something, at least saying something holy?

But it is the voice of God within that brings calm and direction. It drains the negative energy out of the present so that we can go on, calmly aware that there is nowhere where we are alone.

This kind of prayer prepares us to feel the presence of God everywhere because we have discovered that the presence of God is within. It enables us to respond to it in waves of trust that carry us far beyond the storms of the present to the fullness of the future.

**MANTRA:** *Give me the grace to be quiet, to listen for your voice in my heart.*

God said, "Go out and stand on the mountain in the presence of YHWH, for YHWH is about to pass by." Then a great and powerful wind tore the mountain apart and shattered the rocks by YHWH's power—but YHWH was not in the whirlwind. After the wind there was an earthquake—but YHWH was not in the earthquake. After the earthquake came a fire—but YHWH was not in the fire. And after the fire came a gentle whisper. When Elijah heard it, he pulled his cloak over his face and went out and stood at the mouth of the cave. Then a voice said to him, "What are you doing here, Elijah?"

❧ I KINGS 19:11–13

# 11. Vulnerability

*The only true prerequisite for prayer is a broken heart.*  ❧ HASIDIC WISDOM

"I desire to learn how to pray," the disciple said to the Holy One. "Then here is how," the Holy One said as he plunged the head of the disciple into a bucket of water and held it there while the disciple struggled to be free. "Why did you do a thing like that?" the disciple demanded to know as he came up out of the water gasping for breath. "In order to teach you," the Holy One said, "that when you get to the point where you know you need God as much as you need air, you will have learned how to pray."

The point is a good one. When we have everything we need in life, it is often difficult to want God, too. It is even more difficult to know how much we need God.

Only when the foundations of our precarious life have been shaken can we realize that we are not worlds unto ourselves. Only then can we ever really discover that the spiritual life is a basic of life, not an accoutrement.

Until then, God is a possibility—even a probability, perhaps—but God is not yet the air we breathe, the song we sing, the life we seek. After all, we run on the wind of our own energy. We breathe the air of our own making. We sing songs that confirm the glory of the self.

We have everything, why would we look for more? In fact, what more is there?

The truth is that it is pain and need and vulnerability that lead us directly to God. Then we do not need to practice prayer. We become a prayer. We throw ourselves on the heart of God. We look for the balm that does not exist in the world as we know it. Then we trust our lives to our only salvation—the love and mercy of God.

When pain comes that is bigger than anything we can deal with by ourselves, we begin to look beyond the superficial to the spiritual for answers. When we lose what we thought was our everything, we begin to find that only Everything is everything.

When there are no words that can possibly describe the depth and breadth of our pain, we discover that only God can fill such deadening emptiness. When our hearts have finally broken open, when our invincibility breaks down, when we can no longer adore at the shrines to the self, material or physical, then and only then can God really come in. Then and only then will we discover both what it is to pray and what is worth praying for.

**MANTRA:** *Great God, give me the experience of your presence in pain so that I can give myself entirely to you.*

Then Jesus called out in a loud voice, "Lazarus, come out!" And Lazarus came out of the tomb, still bound hand and foot with linen strips, his face wrapped in a cloth....Many of those who had come to console Martha and Mary, and saw what Jesus did, put their faith in him.

✣ JOHN 11:43–45

# 12. Gratitude

*If the only prayer you say in your life is "thank you," that would suffice.*

❧ MEISTER ECKHART

Gratitude is not only the posture of praise but it is also the basic element of real belief in God.

When we bow our heads in gratitude, we acknowledge that the works of God are good. We recognize that we cannot, of ourselves, save ourselves. We proclaim that our existence and all its goods come not from our own devices but are part of the works of God. Gratitude is the alleluia to existence, the praise that thunders through the universe as tribute to the ongoing presence of God with us even now.

Thank you for the new day.

Thank you for this work.

Thank you for this family.

Thank you for our daily bread.

Thank you for this storm and the moisture it brings to a parched earth.

Thank you for the corrections that bring me to growth.

Thank you for the bank of crown vetch that brings color to the hillside.

Thank you for the pets that bind us to nature.

Thank you for the necessities that keep me aware of your bounty in my life.

Without doubt, unstinting gratitude saves us from the sense of self-sufficiency that leads to forgetfulness of God.

Praise is not an idle virtue in life. It says to us, "Remember to whom you are indebted. If you never know need, you will come to know neither who God is nor who you yourself are."

Need is what tests our trust. It gives us the opportunity to allow others to hold us up in our weakness, to realize that only God in the end is the measure of our fullness.

Once we know need we are better human beings. For the first time we know solidarity with the poorest of the poor. We become owners of the pain of the world and devote ourselves to working in behalf of those who suffer.

Finally, it is need that shows us how little it takes to be happy.

Once we know all of those things we have come face-to-face with both creation and the Creator. It is the alleluia moment that discovers both God and goodness for us.

Let us learn to come to prayer with an alleluia heart so that our prayer can be sincere.

**MANTRA:** *Praise to you, O God. Let all creation sing your praise.*

My soul proclaims your greatness, O God, and my spirit rejoices in you, my Savior.

🌿 LUKE 1:46–47

# 13. Routine

*Prayer is the key of the morning and the bolt of the evening.* ❧ GANDHI

Routine, the almost thoughtless doing of the endless repetitions of life—is one of the mainstays of human development. It saves us from the cross of chaos that plagues any life that lacks shape and form. It ties us to the earth and liberates us from a sense of eternal free fall.

Because we know what we will do every Tuesday night, every day from 9:00 to 5:00, every Friday after work, we are free to think about other things. We can concentrate on the substance of life if we are not in a state of constant uncertainty. Confusion about what to do next, where to do it, with whom to discuss it, how long it will take, disorients the soul.

By setting up schedules and timetables, we assure ourselves that what needs to be done will be done. Then, we can attend to all the other things that happen without warning: the telephone calls and drop-in visitors, the sick child and the crashed computer, the new idea and the old project.

The very dailiness of prayer does for us what nothing else can do: It encapsulates us in a sense of human purpose. It gives us a star to steer by that never fades.

Morning prayer done every day, consciously and contemplatively, defines the attitudes we will take into the day with us. It gives us a framework for looking at life that gets behind the burden of the day to come and the warnings of impending disaster that come with the morning news. It takes us to the source of what it will take to sustain us as we go. It refreshes the sense of spiritual resolve in us day after day after day. It gives us a vision beyond the humdrum to the meaning of why we do what we do.

Morning prayer is, indeed, the key, to being able to face not only what will come but the way we deal with it, as well.

Evening prayer washes away the dross of the day. It brings us to peace with ourselves. Despite the struggles of the day that are still pending, still waiting for us tomorrow again, it blesses the efforts of this day and promises blessing for the next. It closes the door on this day so that we can open the door on the next with hope and with welcome.

It confirms in us a sense that the God who made us also knows the dust from which we come. And loves it. And believes in it. And will be with us in all the struggles it brings again tomorrow.

It is the routine of daily prayer that carries us from one day to the other, full of trust, followed by mercy.

**MANTRA: *Great God, bless my rising and sleeping so that I may live faithful to your love.***

Now I can lie down and sleep,
    and then awake again,
for you have hold of me—
no fear now of those tens of thousands who
    stand against me wherever I turn.
Arise, YHWH!               *PSALM 3:6–7

# 14. Prayerfulness

*Prayer is not a discourse. It is a form of life, the life with God. That is why it is not confined to the moment of verbal statement.* ❧ JACQUES ELLUL

Saying prayers and being prayerful are two different things. Saying prayers has to do with following a prayer pattern. We say a prayer for those who are sick. We pray for "special intentions." We say special prayers to mark special moments in life: the baptism of a child, the celebration of Easter, the blessing of a marriage, the beginning of a new work or project or time of life.

Many of the prayers we say have been passed down to us for generations. The psalms, for instance, mark the cry of the human spirit across time. The Scriptures speak of peoples and prayers over twenty centuries before us. Prayers such as these in every culture carry the wisdom of the past to enlighten the insights of the present.

These prayers are venerable, a history of the unchanging human spirit. But they do not guarantee that those who say them will ever be really "prayerful" people. They tell us only that people pray.

Prayerfulness, on the other hand, is the capacity to walk in touch with God through everything in life. It is the internal awareness that God is with me—now, here, in this, always. It is an awareness of the continuing presence of God. It is my dialogue with the living God who inhabits my world in Spirit and in Mind.

Prayerfulness sees God everywhere.

Prayerfulness talks to God everywhere.

Prayerfulness submits the uncertainties of the moment to the scrutiny of the internal eye of God. It trusts that no matter how malevolent the situation may be, I can walk through it unharmed because God is with me.

Prayerfulness is both gift and grace, both a natural disposition and a quality of soul to be developed. But what develops it?

Prayerfulness is fostered by the simple consciousness that God is. That God is near us at all times.

That God is closer to us than the breath we breathe. That God is available, a silence in the midst of chaos, a voice in the midst of confusion, a promise at the center of the tumult.

If I ask and I listen and I reach out and I fill my heart with the words of the One who is the Word, then I will be answered. Somehow the path will become clear.

Prayerfulness is the capacity to live intensely involved in the world and intensely immersed with the God who made it at the same time. It is a way of life that is aware of all of it in all its forms—both spiritual and material—at once.

**MANTRA:** *Great God, give me a continuing awareness of your voice in my heart, your will in my mind.*

Those who love me will be true to my word, and Abba God will love them; and we will come to them and make our dwelling place with them.

✤ JOHN 14:23

# 15. Acceptance

*That's our Lord's will…that our prayers
and our trust be alike: large.*

❧ JULIAN OF NORWICH

We like to think that we know what's good
for us. The right to take charge of our own
lives is a rite of passage not to be denied. "It's her
choice," we like to say. "She'll have to live with it."
True.

The problem is that the desire to control our own
lives often does as much to corrupt our spiritual
lives as it seems to do to enhance our personal ones.
It's one thing to set out to order a future we have de-
termined for ourselves. It is entirely another to set
out to govern God.

But the path to real prayer is a history of a lot of
our attempts to do just that.

"I prayed for months," we say, "but he left me anyway."

"I fasted every Wednesday for a year," we muse, "but she died anyway and I was left with five kids to raise."

"I went to church every Sunday and gave twice what I could afford to the church," we moan, "and still was not accepted at graduate school."

But when we look back, we see clearly that the life that followed the divorce was clearly better than the one we'd had. Or that the second marriage was at least as good as the first. Or that I would never have been as happy doing medicine as I have been doing counseling.

Teresa of Avila puts it this way: "There are more tears shed over answered prayers," she says, "than over unanswered prayers." Sometimes, we get what we want and find out we're miserable with it. Sometimes, we get what we didn't want, and finally realize that it was the far better thing for me than my own choice could ever have been.

Prayer is the gift of being able to put my life into the hands of God—and trust the path that opens before me. Whether I think I would have wanted it or not.

After all, if God is with me, what real difference does it make in the end how I get to where I'm going? It's never what I do that counts. It's who I become because of what I do which, in the end, is the real measure of the beauty of my life.

**MANTRA:** *Loving God, give me the grace to accept the fact that the path I'm on will, eventually, bring me home both to myself and to you.*

Give us today our daily bread.

❧ MATTHEW 6:11

# 16. Patience

*The greatest prayer is patience.*

◆ BUDDHA

"There was a time," the story goes, "when, if a person missed a stagecoach, that was no problem. They just waited for the next one to come through six months later. Now, in our time," the wag says, "people have a breakdown if they miss one section of a revolving door." The story makes a point worth considering. The problem is that in speeding up our society, we too often fail to realize that life is about more than speed—especially the spiritual life.

The spiritual life is a process of growing into maturity one mistake, one unsuccessful effort at a time, until we finally realize that there is no such thing as a spiritual mistake. All we need to do to turn them all into gain is to learn from them.

Prayer and prayerfulness help us to understand that process is as important to the quality of life as productivity is. The way we go about life is as important to its outcome as what we do with ourselves in the course of it. The fact is that very few things can really be forced before their time. Love cannot be forced. Growth cannot be forced. Understanding cannot be forced. Acceptance cannot be forced. Like birth, those things germinate in darkness until ripeness comes—either in them or in us.

Coming to appreciate the difference between God's time and our time is essential to becoming spiritual people. God's time is what prepares us to function well in our time.

It is easy, for instance, to be "spiritual" when nothing deters us or tests our spirit or tries our hearts. But it is precisely the experience of being discouraged in our efforts that may strengthen us enough to deal well with whatever it is for which we wait. It is testing our spirits—having to check our impulses over and over again, that finally teaches us to control our anger or damp our lusts. It is the pain of loss that teaches us that nothing is ever lost; it is only to be found in other ways.

To live the God-life means learning to "compose our souls in patience," as the ancients called it. It means learning to wait for God's good time for all our needs to be answered—somehow, for all our desires to be satisfied—somehow, for all our hopes to be fulfilled—somehow, though not necessarily, the way we ourselves would have done.

Prepare, prepare, prepare. And then wait. In God's good time, God's will, will come.

**MANTRA:** *All-knowing God, give me what I need but only when you know that I am ready to receive it.*

When the designated time had come, God sent forth the Christ—born of a woman, born under the Law—to deliver from the law those who were subjected to it.    ❧ GALATIANS 4:4

# 17. Change

*Prayer is not just spending time with God....If it ends there, it is fruitless. No, prayer is dynamic. Authentic prayer changes us—unmasks us.*

❧ TERESA OF AVILA

To wait for God does not mean that there is nothing else for me to do in the spiritual life than pray. Prayer is not a cocoon. We do not simply go into prayer and hope to come out on the other end of the exercise fully grown in the Spirit, perfectly new, totally finished. All dross removed. All rust scoured. The soul burnished. The heart refurbished. The soul bright and radiant. The mind clear and certain.

Not at all. There is too much of us in us to ever disappear. Nor is it meant to. No, the function of prayer is not to obliviate the self. It is to become to the utmost what we are meant to be no matter what situation we are in. Prayer is the process that leads us to become what Jesus models for us to be.

To pray does not mean that we will cease to be ourselves. It simply means that we will come to know clearly what it will take to become more of the Jesus figure we are all meant to be.

Prayer confronts us with ourselves and measures the distance between who and what we are and who and what Jesus is.

We watch Jesus confront the leaders of the day. He calls the priests and Pharisees to cleanse the temple and lift from the backs of the people the laws of the synagogue that burden them. He calls the leaders of the state to stop living off the backs of the poor. And he calls us to do the same.

We listen to Jesus jeopardize his social approval, risk his very life by speaking out in public against the oppression of people in both synagogue and state. And he calls us to do the same.

Being immersed in prayer, really immersed in prayer, sears our souls. It forces us to see how far from our own ideals we stand. It challenges the images of goodness and piety and integrity we project. It confronts us with what it really means to live a good life. It requires courage of us rather than simply piety.

It says again and again, "Come, follow me."

It is in following Jesus down from the mountaintop, along the roads of the world, through the public parts of the city, into the ghettoes of the poor and the halls of government and the chanceries of the churches, saying with John the Baptist, "Repent and sin no more" that prayer gets its hallmark of undisputed credibility.

**MANTRA:** *Redeeming God, give me the courage to change myself so that I can be for others what you call me to be.*

Your attitude must be the same as that of Christ Jesus: Christ, though in the image of God, didn't deem equality with God something to be clung to—but instead became completely empty and took on the image of oppressed humankind.... ❦ PHILIPPIANS 2:5–7

# 18. Consciousness

*Certain thoughts are prayers. There are*
*moments when, whatever be the attitude*
*of the body, the soul is on its knees.*

❧ VICTOR HUGO, *LES MISERABLES*

A lifetime of prayer is a lifetime of intimacy with God. That constancy of soulful conjunction, of awareness of the presence within, is a stage of prayer beyond saying prayers. And yet at the same time, it is surely an effect of saying prayers. The One to whom we reach out all our days reaches back to us. The One who has been within reach all our lives has begun to come to life quietly, but clearly, within us. There is no distance anymore.

There is darkness, of course. There is otherness, yes. But there is also the sense of companionship that never goes away.

We are no less ourselves then. But we have come to know and see and respond to life differently. We know now that we are no longer alone. And so, when confronted with the unknown, we turn inwardly and immediately to the source and end of life.

We see now that this life is not the only life we have. There is a rich and deepening life within calling us beyond the transciency of this one to the eternal energy of life beyond it.

We respond to life now on two levels at once: to the demands of this one and in search of guidance, of strength, of direction from the next.

We don't need to kneel anymore to find God outside ourselves. Our souls are in a state of an eternal bow before the presence of God within us.

We live now in a state of consciousness beyond the conscious. We know life to be more than simply the life of the senses. Now there is a soul-life within us that is clear and cognizant. We are now more than our public self. We know that now we live by more than the mandates and customs and ideals of society. We live by the word of God that vibrates within us every minute of the day.

It is the soul now, not the body, that is always at prayer.

**MANTRA:** *God, speak within me always so that I may speak Your word in every dimension of my life.*

Anyone who listens to you, listens to me. Anyone who rejects you, rejects me; and those who reject me, reject the One who sent me.

❧ LUKE 10:16

# 19. Blessing

*You pray in your distress and in your need. Would that you might pray also in the fullness of your joy and in your days of abundance.* ❧ KAHLIL GIBRAN

Life is not meant to be a burden. Life is not a problem to be solved. It is a blessing to be celebrated.

Every dimension of life, its gains and its losses, are reason for celebration because each of them brings us closer to wisdom and fullness of understanding.

From each and every moment of life we learn something that makes us more alive because we are now more knowing than we were before. Loss and loneliness, darkness and depression all sear the soul and cleanse it of its sense of self-sufficiency. Suffering directs it to the God of life.

But so does bounty and beauty and abundance. These give us a foretaste of wholeness. These are the palpable manifestations of the goodness of God in our lives. Both of these things come unbidden. They are not signs of either our sin or our sinlessness. They are simply signs that the God of life is a living, loving God.

Learning to celebrate joy is one of the great practices of the spiritual life. It confirms our trust in God. It affirms the greatness of creation. It seals our dependence on God. It attests to the beauty of the present and asserts our confidence in the beauty of the future. It recognizes the mercy and love of God.

Every year in celebrating our birthdays and the birthdays of those we love we are called to remember the gift of life itself. We take time out to ask ourselves what we have done with our lives, what we have done for others with our lives. We see again the potential of every single life in the world.

When we celebrate the good things in life, we trace them to the Creator who gives without merit, openhandedly, out of the very goodness of community, love, and support that are by nature at the base of the human condition.

Joy gives us strength for the unknown. It leads us into the emptiness of life with hope in the God of surprises and with a smile on our faces.

**MANTRA:** *Loving God, give me the grace to find joy where I am and to celebrate it always.*

But let all who take refuge in you be glad and rejoice forever. Protect them, so that those who love your Name will rejoice in you. As for the just, YHWH, you surround them with the shield of your will. ✢ PSALM 5:11–12

# 20. Awareness

*Wherever you turn, there is the face of
God.*  MUHAMMED

Once upon a time a Sufi made the annual
pilgrimage to Mecca. It was a long walk for
him and the sun was high. He had come miles
without stopping. Finally, in the sight of the mosque
at Mecca, sure of the goal now, the old man lay
down in the road to rest.

Suddenly, one of the other pilgrims shook
him awake, rough and harsh in the doing of it.
"Wake up," he commanded. "You blaspheme. You
lie in such a way that your feet are pointed toward
God in the holy mosque! What kind of Sufi are
you?!"

The old Sufi opened one eye, smiled a bit, and
said, "I thank you, holy sir. Now if you would be

kind enough to turn my feet in some direction where they are not pointed toward God."

When we still believe that prayer in church is better than prayer on the street, or the bus, or the beach, or the job, we have yet to understand the omnipresence of God. We have yet to become aware that God is with us wherever we go, whatever we are doing.

By punctuating every day with a round of choral prayer, the monastic lives in an atmosphere designed to cultivate continual awareness of the presence of God. At one time, when chiming clocks were a feature of every room, a simple sentence said as the clock marked the changing of the hour, maintained the practice.

Prayer, regular and rote, is a bridge to awareness. Morning and evening prayer, prayer before and after meals, prayer as we begin a journey, private prayers at the beginning of every major task, all call us to remember what it is that sustains us in life.

But whatever our devices for calling ourselves to some kind of formal recognition of the place of God in our lives—a cross on a lapel, a statue on the mantle, a picture on a wall, a rosary on the way to work—it is also true that awareness is the foundation of prayerfulness. Otherwise we can say prayers under regular and common conditions and still ignore the meaning of them. We can make the prayer itself God instead of making God the ground of our lives.

The secret lies in asking ourselves one simple question at every pause point in our lives: What is my life all about? When we get to the point where the answer to that question is always and everywhere, "it is about my life in God," we are already there.

**MANTRA:** *God of life, live in my heart so that everything I see speaks to me of you.*

That same night God appeared to him and said, "I am the God of your father Abraham. Don't be afraid, for I am with you. I will bless you."

❧ GENESIS 26:24

# 21. Growth

*To insist on a spiritual practice that served you in the past is to carry the raft on your back after you have crossed the river.*

✦ BUDDHA

Every step of the spiritual way is the way. To cement our souls in one step of the way at the expense of all the others is to doom ourselves to a life of spiritual childhood. Until each of the attitudes we bring to prayer comes to maturity, we stand to suspend the process of our own progress in the spiritual life.

The problem is that we are inclined to forget that the way to spiritual adulthood is a long one. It is a journey of many stages. It is a quest of multiple parts. It is never static and it cannot be trussed to any one point or bound to any place, or committed to any one particular practice in the spiritual lexicon. If it is, then that practice has failed us—or we are failing it. "When I was a child," Paul says, "I thought like a child....When I became an adult, I put an end to that." The story is a common one—in every aspect of life. It speaks of trial and failure, of insight and wisdom, of stretching the self to full growth at great cost.

There is no dimension of life in which we expect to be the same kind of person at fifty that we were at thirty. No one expects to think the same about the world at forty-five as they did at eighteen. No one expects to know the same degree of information about life at sixty-five as they did at thirty-five. Why then would we expect our spiritual lives to fossilize, to be at their ultimate, at the age of eighteen?

The practices we learned in childhood spoke to the child in us: Christmas was about the birth of the baby Jesus; Lent was about giving up candy; Jonah was really swallowed by a whale. All those stories taught us about the faith—but they did not teach us the whole faith. Coming to realize that Christmas is about the presence of the divine in our midst is a matter of maturing in the real message of the faith. Lent is about owning the weakness in ourselves as we remember the weakness of those who betrayed Jesus before us. Jonah was caught up in the evil forces around him—just as we are, despite the fact that we profess a commitment to God.

Sometime in life, we have to give up the manger and move on to the cross. At some point in life, we need to leave the satisfaction of rituals for the sake of surrender to the God-life to which we are called.

Otherwise, we never grow in the faith. We choose to live at a level of spiritual childhood despite our commitment to grow into God from age to age.

**MANTRA:** *God of life, enable us to grow into you from age to age until the fullness of time makes us spiritually whole.*

When I was a child, I used to speak like a child, think like a child, reason like a child. But when I became an adult, I put childish ways aside.

❧ 1 CORINTHIANS 13:11

# 22. Immersion

*When you are in love with someone, it seems that the face of the beloved is before you when you drive, when you type, when you are taking out insurance....Somehow or other we can encompass these two realities—the face of the beloved and whatever we happen to be doing. Prayer is like that.*

❧ CATHERINE DE HUECK DOHERTY

We have been told for so long that the world is made up of two distinct planes—earth and heaven, the material and the spiritual, the rational and the mystical, that we have come to believe it. The interesting thing is that we know inside ourselves that such distinct division is simply not true.

After the death of a parent, for instance, as time

goes by and the initial shock of the loss wears off, we begin to hear their voices again. "Every time I do that, I can hear my mother telling me to be sensible," we say with a kind of quiet smile. We joke about it. We laugh at ourselves about it. But, nevertheless, we know that it is true. We do live in two different kinds of worlds—the mystical and the material, the physical and the real—but we also know that the overlap between them is just as true, just as real.

The purpose of prayer is to bring us deeper and deeper into the center of the intersection between the two of them. To fail to be wholly present to the marriage of the mystical and material can smack of psychological imbalance.

Prayer provides the consciousness that leads to immersion in the reality to which it points. It speaks to us of higher ideals, of another realm of existence beyond success and wealth and power. It brings us face-to-face with the purpose of creation, the foundations of truly developed life.

Prayer is the memory of the Beloved, the filter, the scrim, through which we begin to see all reality, all life, all decisions, all purposes and all goals.

To come to immersion in God we must come to immersion in prayer. We must submerse ourselves in thoughts of the God within, the God who calls us out of ourselves and beyond ourselves and, at the same time, ever deeper and deeper within to connect with the real substance of Life.

Prayer tells us that there is more to life than what life shows us on the surface of it. There is eternal love that lasts beyond momentary passion. There are the questions of the meaning of life that supersede the desire for mere satiation with life. There is the hot and burning consciousness that every life, my life, has a purpose beyond the simple living of it that can be realized only by extending myself beyond it.

Scripture is clear that Jesus appeared to many after the Resurrection who had followed him. But if that is so, then, why not, after years of our own immersion in him, does he not rise to the most profound part of our hearts now?

**MANTRA:** *Great God, stretch me beyond myself to the point where you wait for me in quiet.*

After that, he was seen by more than five hundred sisters and brothers at once, most of whom are still alive, although some have fallen asleep.  ❧ 1 CORINTHIANS 15:6

# 23. Righteousness

*The guarantee of one's prayer is not in saying a lot of words. The guarantee of one's petition is very easy to know: How do I treat the poor? Because that is where God is.*

❧ ARCHBISHOP OSCAR ROMERO

The question Archbishop Romero puts before us is a fundamental one: How shall we know if all the praying we do is a truly effective spiritual practice?

What's it all about? How do we know? How can anyone know if we are really people of prayer or only people who pray?

And the answer Romero gives is a clear one: It all depends, he says, on how it affects the way we treat others. Especially the poorest of the poor, the ones who have no hold on us. The ones who have nothing to give us for doing it. The mass of anonymous ones who have no place in our social circles, no boon to bestow on us in public, nothing whatsoever to add to our own circumstances, social or personal, as we go through life.

Which biblical model do we bring to the practice of praying: Dives, the rich man, who prays but ignores the cry of the poor asking to eat the crumbs from his table? Or Lazarus, the poor man, who has nothing in this life but whose needs, in the end, are heard by God? Dives spends eternity in Gehenna. Lazarus spends eternity in the lap of God.

The question is: Which of these two figures became the prayers they prayed? And what is that saying to us about the value and merit of our own lives? The effectiveness of our own prayers to bring us to the fullness of ourselves? To unmask our own selfishness? To make us builders of the kingdom?

The point of prayer is not to spend our prayer lives begging for ourselves but to turn us into the Jesus figures who answer the prayers of others.

Prayer is meant to so change our self-centeredness into community that having prayed in the Our

Father, "thy kingdom come, they will be done," we spend our lives doing something to bring it.

Prayer opens us to ourselves. It exposes our weaknesses. It enlarges our vision of the purpose of life. It dins into us the word of God. It unmasks our own needs. It calls us to become the rest of ourselves.

**MANTRA:** *Merciful God, make me an instrument of your mercy. Give me the courage to do your will so that others may live.*

Once there was a rich person who dressed in purple and linen and feasted splendidly every day. At the gate of this person's estate lay a beggar named Lazarus, who was covered with sores. Lazarus longed to eat the scraps that fell from the rich person's table, and even the dogs came and licked Lazarus' sores. One day poor Lazarus died and was carried by the angels to the arms of Sarah and Abraham. The rich person likewise died and was buried. In Hades, in torment, the rich person looked up and saw Sarah and Abraham in the distance, and Lazarus resting in their company.

"Sarah and Abraham," the rich person cried, "have pity on me! Send Lazarus to dip the tip of his finger in water and cool off my tongue, for I am tortured by these flames!" But they said, "My child, remember that you were well off in your lifetime, while Lazarus was in misery. Now Lazarus has found consolation here, and you have found torment." ❧ LUKE 16:19–25

# 24. Responsibility

*Prayer consists for the most part in insisting that God do for us what we are unwilling to do for one another. Resolve: Let's do for one another what we would have God do for us. This is known as God-like activity.*  ❧ DAN BERRIGAN, SJ

Our ideas of God determine our ideas of prayer. If God is the source of life, if we are "made in God's image," and we are meant to will for the world what God wills for the world, then we pray one way. If, on the other hand, God is that great cornucopia in the sky, who doles out life to us a piece at a time—if we beg for it correctly—then we pray another way entirely.

But God is not a magician. God is not a vending machine. God is the fullness of life, the magnet of our hearts, the model and purpose and end of all our actions. We are here to continue what God has begun: the growing of the garden of life.

The way we pray determines whether our faith is true or false. The way we pray measures whether our piety is childish or mature.

False piety settles down, prayer book in hand, to wheedle God into doing what we feel must be done. False piety bargains with God: I will go to church every day if you will…I will give money to charity if you will…I will stop smoking if you will….

People who negotiate with God are like children who say, "If I take the garbage out every day, then can I go to the party?" The whole notion of the purpose of prayer as the development of a relationship with God escapes them.

These are people who feel like pawns in the universe, barely human at all, totally powerless. Their whole notion of moral agency is to be "good" so that they can wrest from God what they do not take steps to get for themselves.

They live on a shallow faith iced over with a thin layer of piety. They have missed the point that piety is the practice of spiritual disciplines intended to deepen our awareness of God in life, not to turn God into a mirage, a distant idol.

The question for faith is not, Does God bless us? The question is whether or not the purpose of prayer is to coax God into getting things for us or to give us the strength it will take to deal with whether we get them or not.

It is not faith to rely on God to supply what we are capable of doing for ourselves. Faith is not passivity. Faith is the surety that if we are meant to have what we are striving for that it will come in God's good time—as long as we do our part, as well, to make it possible.

**MANTRA:** *Faithful God, give me the strength to work for the fullness of creation so that your will may be done on earth as it is in heaven.*

Seek first God's reign, and God's justice, and all these things will be given to you besides.

✤ MATTHEW 6:33

# 25. Intimacy

*When you pray, don't behave like the hypocrites; they love to pray standing up in synagogues and on street corners for people to see them....When you pray, go to your room, shut the door, and pray to God who is in that secret place.*

MATTHEW 6:5–6

There is a very important public aspect to prayer. The rituals of any community—secular or sacred—serve to glue a group together. They form a common tradition, a universal mind, a sense of belonging, a social system far deeper and longer lasting than any government can be without them.

The story goes that when Peter the Great set out to unite the country of Russia, he sent emissaries from one place to another to examine their religions in order to determine which of these would best fit the Russian people. Without a state religion, he argued, no amount of government could hold the country together.

But however central hymns or public worship may be to the public identity of the group, they are no substitute for the faith development that is of the essence of personal prayer. On the contrary.

Public displays of faith may actually have very little to do with real faith at all. In fact, it may actually be nothing more than a free pass to a reputation for goodness. It may be nothing more than public facade, no sure measure of a person's spiritual depth at all. Only intimacy with God can do that.

It is only in the privacy of our hearts that we fully unmask the self—even to the self. There we are able, knowing ourselves, to surrender that knowledge to God for healing, for strengthening of our commitment, for the insight and wisdom it will take to go on.

Private prayer is the only genuine path to real intimacy with God. In private prayer we allow God to know us and we come to know God differently than distance or pomp or public rituals can ever allow.

Public prayer always presents us with the temptation to make our God either the place or the people with whom we pray. With all its grandeur and satisfaction it can seduce us to believe that because there is prayer here, this place—these people—must be good. This kind of prayer can make religion itself an idol. Blinded by commitment to the group or the splendor of the place or the moral security that comes with being "obedient" to a system, we find cults and holy wars great and glorious things.

Only in the intimacy of the heart, steeped in the words of the One who is mercy and goodness, justice and peace, can we see clearly the laws we are really meant to follow, the life we are truly meant to live.

Then we come to realize that we all come into this world alone and we leave it the same way. There is no group, however strong their hold on our obedience, who, in the end, will go with us to the bar of conscience.

And it is conscience, not systems, that private prayer is really meant to be about.

**MANTRA:** *Form in me, O God, a pure heart. Lead me to yourself alone.*

When you pray, don't behave like the hypocrites; they love to pray standing up in synagogues and on street corners for people to see them....When you pray, go to your room, shut the door, and pray to God who is in that secret place. ❧ MATTHEW 6:5–6

# 26. Inwardness

*Pray inwardly even if you do not enjoy it. It does good, though you feel nothing. Yes, even though you think you are doing nothing.* ❧ JULIAN OF NORWICH

We live in a world that is constantly pulling us out of ourselves to replace the inner life with virtual reality. We live other people's lives now—characters in television soap operas, continuing story lines in serial dramas, celebrities on game shows, sports figures on and off the field, reality shows that make voyeurs of us all. The inward life is a thing of the past—or, if not completely past, not completely comfortable.

The first thing the novice learns about the process of praying is the process of sitting still, of doing nothing, of learning to become aware of the chaos inside of us instead of filling it with the chaos outside of us. It is the chaos inside of us that is the beginning of a relationship with God. It is here that the stuff of our unrest, our ambition, our narcissism, our confusion lurks. And so, it is here that we must begin to understand the real undertow that is constant within us. It is here that we will find and name the real fears, the deepest hopes, the fullest feelings of life.

No, this soul-wrestling does not feel good. But feeling and fidelity are not the same thing. Feeling tells us where we do not want to be. Fidelity tells us that to grow we must stay where we need to be. It is what does not feel good about the raging silence that is exactly what must be tamed if we are ever to grow beyond the self into the arms of God.

There is no finding God, however, until we manage at last to listen to the silence, to rest naked before God, to come to peace with the self.

Fidelity, the continuing conviction that God is what waits for us at the deepest part of our inner self is what keeps us at the taming of the storms however long the process may take.

But without fidelity to the process of inwardness—the willingness to withdraw from the plastic noises around us, to learn the sounds of silence that are the call of God—the real good can never come. The call to a life beyond internal chaos, the shaping of newer, richer, more substantial ideas, the focus of the soul on God, the breaking of the chains that come with being captive to the superficial—are the bounty of the inward life.

It is the inward life that makes us free to be our real, total selves. It makes us free for a relationship with God.

**MANTRA:** *Lead me beyond the chaos within myself, O God, so I may find where you hide in my heart.*

YHWH, my God, you are the One I seek.
  My soul thirsts for you,
  my body longs for you
  in this dry and weary land
  where there is no water.      ❧ PSALM 63:1

# 27. Formlessness

*Many winding roads and paths lead to the top of the mountain, but at the peak we all gaze at the single bright moon.* ⚜ IKKYU

It is so easy to be seduced, even by the good. But once it happens we stand to lose the very gain the finding of the good should have given us.

We find a prayer form that satisfies, even uplifts our spirits, often brings us to a new level of awareness and enlightenment. Everything is going well until the prayer form itself becomes our God.

If I can't pray every day in this pew at this time, the day is disturbed.

If I can't sing this hymn on this feast in this place, the feast has failed me.

If someone changes the translation of the "Our Father," I can't concentrate on it.

If someone uses universal language for God rather than male pronouns, I get angry.

If there are no candles, no incense, no flowers and bright clothes and robes, it can't possibly be real prayer.

Though those things are all good, all important at some time in some circumstances, none of them is a worthy substitute for God. In fact, the very fact of needing to have them—at whatever cost to anyone else—may be the real sign of how little we've learned about God while doing them.

Just as we change as we go through life, so must our prayer forms change in order to nourish the new growth the last phase of our spiritual journey planted in us.

When we stop in the course of the spiritual journey declaring that we have already achieved the end of our search—that we have found the God for whom we seek—it is doubtful that we have found anything more than our own comfort, our own will, the god we have made for ourselves out of our own image. And that is a puny God indeed.

Once we begin a real spiritual journey we will be led from prayer point to prayer point, deeper and deeper into the Mystery that is God. We will be expected to let go so that God can lead us now. And that path has no end.

**MANTRA:** *Give me the grace to let go, O God, so that by not finding you I am able to discover you more.*

Like newborn babies, be hungry for nothing but milk—the pure milk of the word that will make you grow into salvation, now that you have "tasted that our God is good."

*❧ I PETER 2:2–3*

# 28. Purpose

*Forever at God's door*
*I gave my heart and soul.*
*My fortune, too.*
*I've no flock anymore,*
*no other work in view.*
*My occupation: love.*
*It's all I do.*

❦ JOHN OF THE CROSS

The purpose of prayer is not prayer. The purpose of prayer is to come to love God as much as possible with all the insights into the nature and presence of God this world allows.

In fact, one of the most consistent themes in mystical literature is the clear notion that the Mystic is not seeking spiritual escape from the life of the world. The mystic, history records in one life after another of them, is simply seeking God. The life of those who practice prayer deeply and regularly is clearly a life of enlightenment. They come to know both the mind of God and the obstacles of their own hearts with an acuity uncommon even to the professional bearers of the tradition—its ministers and officers, its scholars and its priests.

What they do not seek are "consolations" in prayer.

To strive for spiritual "consolations," the ancients taught, meant the desire of the seeker to find the spiritual life "rewarding," pleasant, easy, comforting. It was the desire to have ecstatic experiences. It was the hope of being lifted up out of the self to the point of the ethereal. It was, consciously or unconsciously, the hope to use prayer as an escape. In some traditions, drugs and a kind of self-hypnosis are used to enhance the chances of dissolving into some kind of other-worldly trance.

But it was not the way of the genuine mystic. Some of them, in fact—John of the Cross, Teresa of Avila—suffered even more in prayer at the thought of the sufferings of Jesus or the awareness of the suffering of others, than most of their contemporaries did who never fully followed a life of prayer at all.

Some of them lived in spiritual dryness—"the dark night of the soul"—all their lives.

So what was their prayer life about? It was just like mine and yours. It was about learning, as I did, what the catechism said, "to know and love God with all our hearts, all our mind, and all our strength."

Prayer is effort on my part and depth of life and fullness of understanding on God's part.

God does surely come to us in prayer. In fact, in prayer we are seeking the God who is seeking us. This same God spoke in dreams, and as Hildegard of Bingen said, "in mental visions" to the people of God throughout the ages. That same God is surely speaking to us, as well. Prayer is the process of learning to listen.

**MANTRA:** *Let me know you, O God. Let me know you and love you with all my heart, all my mind and all my strength.*

But I, because of your great love,
    will enter your house;
I will worship in your holy temple
    in awe and reverence.    ❧ PSALM 5:7

# 29. Abandonment

*Pure love and prayer are learned in the hour when prayer has become impossible and your heart has turned to stone.*

                ❧ THOMAS MERTON

P rayer is not an analgesic designed to protect us from life. It is, more times than not, part of the problem of life. One day, we simply don't feel like praying. The next day, we pray but it doesn't make any difference: things do not turn out the way we want them. We try to pray but we're far too distracted by the issues at hand than we are soothed by the quiet or comforted by a sense of the presence of God.

If truth were told, young enthusiasm for the spiritual life dies easily and early. Then, one day we admit to ourselves the truth of the dampening of the spirit:

We haven't had a sense of the presence of God for a long time now—years. We just keep getting up and going through the routine. At first, it was alive with possibility and promise. Then—now—it is more of the same. I'm not changing, my world is not changing, nothing seems different from the days when I didn't pray at all.

So, is it over? Was it ever really real?

Only one thing remains. I do know now that there is something else in life that is more than life on the level of the daily.

When I reach that point in my prayer life, there is one attitude yet to be developed, one thing missing in my understanding of prayer, one thing I am learning but may still not believe: The presence of absence is not the absence of presence. Just because I do not feel God's presence does not mean that God is absent. It only means that prayer is not about me anymore. It is about being what I know now that God means me to be.

In fact, absence is as much a proof of the bondedness called "missing you," as it is a fear of distance called "you don't love me." It is the extension of the spirit to full length and depth and form. It is the challenge to learn to trust darkness as well as light.

Whenever I feel lost, I am being brought to remember that God knows exactly where I am. When I feel abandoned, I am challenged to remember that God is energy not solace. When I demand proof of the Spirit, I am being taught, like Mary Magdalene at the tomb, not to cling to presence but to take that presence to others.

When all those things happen, I have finally learned to pray.

**MANTRA:** *Great God, keep my spirit alive and growing into you more and more by the day.*

> Jesus said to her, "Mary!" She turned to him and said, "Rabboni!"—which means "Teacher." Jesus then said, "Don't hold on to me, for I have not yet ascended to Abba God."
>
> ❧ JOHN 20:16–17

# 30. Effort

*"How does a person seek union with God?"* the seeker asked.

*"The harder you seek,"* the teacher said, *"the more distance you create."*

*"So what can I do about that?"*

*"Understand it isn't there,"* the teacher said.

*"Does that mean that God and I are one?"* the seeker asked.

*"Not one. Not two."*

*"But is that possible?"* the seeker asked.

*"The sun and its light, the ocean and the wave, the singer and the song. Not one. Not two."*  ❧ ANTHONY D MELLO, SJ


L ike the seeker in the story, we can go through life going from one thing to another trying, by means of each of them, to get closer to God.

Whole stores now sell prayer techniques: rings for this, oils for that, formulas and positions and chants and prayers all designed to make the distance between us and God less daunting, less dense, more permeable.

But, ironically, in the end, it's not choosing one ancient spiritual discipline over another that will make the difference between consciousness of God and a sense of my isolation in the universe. The truth is that all of the prayer exercises in the world depend on the one same insight: the notion that to seek God is to have God.

To seek God is to find God. What we want we already have. But the having is about becoming rather than possessing. We become more of the God-life within as we become less of the godless around us.

Having God is not a question of capturing God. It is a question of coming to see God everywhere, in everything—and first of all, deep within ourselves.

God within is the voice, in fact, that is calling us to seek more than we are of ourselves alone. The finding depends only on our commitment to seek.

We are always present to the One whose creative energy keeps us in existence. The question is only whether or not God is present to us. Or to put it another way: What God am I worshiping now with such intensity that I have no time left for any other? Is my God power? And if so, have I given myself away to the pursuit of it? Is my God money, and will I do anything—including ignore the God within—to get it? Is my God lust and so do I waste the life-giving passion in me on the tangible and momentary rather than focus my spirit on the eternals of life?

Finding God within is only a matter of refusing to allow anything else to become my God. There is no effort needed to realize that God is hiding where we least expect to find God. God is hiding in the human heart—first of all, my own. It is time to begin within where the voice is already calling me to come.

**MANTRA:** *Loving God, knowing you are here is enough for me. Give me the courage to listen.*

"The truth is, I've found no one in Israel with such great faith…." Then Jesus said to the centurion, "Go home, it will be done just as you believed it would."     ❧ MATTHEW 8:10, 13

# 31. Readiness

*Once upon a time a disciple asked the elder, "Holy One, is there anything I can do to make myself Enlightened?"*

*"As little as you can do to make the sun rise in the morning."*

*"Then of what use," the disciple asked, "are all the spiritual exercises?"*

*"To make sure," the elder said, "that you are not asleep when the sun begins to rise."* ❧ ANTHONY D MELLO, SJ

In a society where fresh bread is baked in minutes and clocks adjust themselves to universal standards, in instantaneous gratification societies where we can have what we want the minute we want it, it is not easy to talk to disciples about the long, slow process of coming to know God. We like everything now. We want the quick fix, the short course, in eternal verities.

But there is no such thing. There is only God's eternal patience and our lifelong conditioning to having everything instantly. Including our own development.

We do not realize that coming to know God has as much to do with coming to know ourselves as it does to anything we know about God. We do not recognize that it is what we are that will determine the nature of the relationship between God and ourselves. And for that to happen, readiness is the key.

To recognize the word of God when it comes, we need to steep ourselves in the word of God that has been given to us already. The Scriptures model for us the life we seek to live. The history of God's people shows us both the challenges we face in walking with God and the issues in ourselves that must be resolved before we will ever be able to meet those challenges.

The development of spiritual disciplines that train our hearts to the sound of God's voice, the regularity of exercises that measure our fidelity to the search and our attention to the inner life, all ready us for the moment when we suddenly arrive where we did not know we were going.

In the end of a well-defined spiritual life, we do not lose our two-ness. We become the echo of the song. We are not forgiven the obligation to seek the light always but we do become a shadow of the light. We are not relieved of the responsibility to navigate the ocean storms of life with faith. But we are carried through it now on longer, stronger waves of trust.

We discover, yes, that we are still two, but we also come to know that we live with a Presence within that we never had before.

**MANTRA:** *Prepare me, O God, to hear your word, to live your word, to grow forever in rhythm with the vibrations of your word.*

On that day you'll know that I am in God, and you are in me, and I am in you. Those who obey the commandments are the ones who love me, and those who love me will be loved by Abba God. I too will love them and will reveal myself to them.
⁓ JOHN 14:20–21

# 32. Involvement

*A rabbi entered a room in his home and saw his son deep in prayer. In the corner stood a cradle with a crying baby. "Son, can't you hear?" the rabbi said, "The baby is crying." The son said, "Oh, Father, I did not hear it because I was lost in God." And the rabbi said, "Son, one who is lost in God sees the very fly crawling up the wall."*

⁂ ABEL HERZERG

Prayer does not make us less aware of the circumstances of life. It makes us even more aware than we ever were before. Why? Because now we see the world as God sees the world. We hear the cry of the poor as God hears the cry of the poor. We are less wrapped up in ourselves, more aware of the needs of others, not more self-centered than ever.

When we are really wrapped up in the aware-ness of the presence of God in ourselves we come to understand that it is of the nature of God who is everywhere to be present to all of us as well as to ourselves. We begin to see ourselves more and more as a member of the human community rather than as a unique and freestanding individual. We know now in a way we have never realized before that we are not a world unto ourselves.

The acuity of the heart of God comes with the awareness of the presence of God. Once God takes over the heart, there is no one—no child of God in any tradition anywhere—who does not have claim to our heart as well as to the heart of God. We become our brother's keeper, our sister's best sup-port. Our own hearts, like God's, begin to beat with a heart for the entire human race.

To use religion or prayer or contemplation or the search for God as an excuse for ignoring the needs of the world is blasphemy. It denies the very God it purports to preach. It practices the idolatry of the self and calls it union with God. It makes immersion in prayer more important than the fruits of prayer.

Such unabashed confusion of prayer makes a farce of prayer itself.

Those who truly seek God become more sensitive to the rest of the world because they become daily more like the God they love, the Spirit that energizes them. They carry for all to see the urgings of the God who impels them to find the God who lives in them and draws them out of themselves at the same time.

**MANTRA:** *Broaden my heart, O God, to receive you and hear you and roam the world as you do, touching it with healing hands.*

You who are poor are blessed, for the reign of God is yours. You who hunger now are blessed, for you'll be filled. You who weep now are blessed, for you'll laugh. You are blessed when people hate you, when they scorn and insult you and spurn your name as evil because of the Chosen One. On the day they do so, rejoice and be glad: your reward will be great in heaven. ᶘ LUKE 6:20–23

# 33. Humility

*I have been driven many times to my knees by the overwhelming conviction that I had absolutely no other place to go.*

*❧ ABRAHAM LINCOLN*

We spend so much of our lives pretending to be God it is often difficult to remember that we aren't. We proclaim it to the office staff, we remind the family of it by the day, we ply friends with stories of our supernatural victories over small children and store clerks and neighbors. Even early in the process when we go to prayer, we take with us the same attitude of the imperious and the agitated. We order people and things to do our bidding and make our worlds perfect. We secretly expect God to do the same. As Aldous Huxley put it, "The Third Petition of the Lord's Prayer is repeated daily by millions who have not the slightest intention of letting anyone's will be done but their own."

But then, somewhere in life, we find ourselves facing walls that will not move. We have a child who needs special care now—and will need special care all their lives. We lose the savings of a lifetime and all the retirement plans go with them. We develop a chronic disease that will not end our life but will certainly limit it severely. We watch the business fail through no fault of our own but so far beyond us there's not a thing we can do to save it.

Now, we find ourselves new people. We have become the spiritual beggars we never before understood. Except that even begging is useless now. And we know it.

So for what do we pray at a time like this? In fact, why bother?

The questions are important ones. It is possible that there is nothing that teaches prayer more quickly, more effectively than having nothing to pray for that can possibly happen. We are lost in the land of nowhere to go but God, not to change the circumstances of our lives but to change our whole attitude about what life is really about.

We learn now in the throes of a heavy heart that

the grace simply to be may be one of the greatest graces of life. We discover in the silent arms of God that it is enough to be loved, to be understood, rather than "saved," from things that are their own kind of salvation.

Sickness saves us from glorifying the cosmetics of life.

Need saves us from isolating ourselves from the rest of the world.

The limitations of others save us from self-centeredness.

Powerlessness saves us from the sickness of arrogance.

Then, when we go to prayer we go, not to be given something but to be quiet, to develop a heartbeat of acceptance, to become the calm that is calming. Humility makes listeners of us. And in listening to everything that happens to us, we find God's word for us.

**MANTRA:** *Give me the grace, O God, to see behind the circumstances of life to the gifts they bring. Give me the vision to receive them gratefully.*

Be still and know that I am God! ❧ PSALM 46:10

# 34. Simplicity

*If the heart wanders or is distracted, bring it back to the point quite gently and replace it tenderly in its Master's presence. And even if you did nothing during the whole of your hour but bring your heart back and place it again in our Lord's presence, though it went away every time you brought it back, your hour will be very well employed.*

❧ ST. FRANCIS DE SALES

One of the most difficult dimensions of beginning to live a life of prayer is to begin it at all.

What can any of us do that will possibly bridge the gap in life between the self and God? And we are not the first to be confused by it all. "Lord, teach us to pray," the apostles said. The answer they got back, though simple to the core of it, is commonly overlooked.

Jesus did not respond to their question with a list of rules or behaviors or rituals or gestures. He did require five attitudes, however:

*"Our Father who art in heaven, hallowed by thy name..."*

The first attitude is that we be aware of the nature of God. God, Jesus says, is to be "hallowed." Revered. Honored. Praised. Seen as the eternal Other. Beyond us. Above us. The One who transcends every sniveling thing of life.

*"Thy kingdom come, thy will be done, on earth as it is in heaven."*

The second attitude Jesus calls for is commitment to the will of God, here and now and forever. We are to form in ourselves the values held by God if we are ever to be completely human.

*"Give us this day our daily bread."*

The third attitude Jesus counsels to the apostles is dependence on God to give us what we need, even when we do not know what it is. Jesus leads us to understand that what comes to us in life that cannot be corrected at that moment is, at that moment, a gift of God—even if unclear to us right now.

*"Forgive us our sins as we forgive those who sin against us."*

The fourth attitude necessary to pray is to recognize our own need for forgiveness. To go to God asking for the grace we refuse others is to break the bond of love to which God binds us as well as to the Godself.

*"And lead us not into temptation but deliver us from evil."*

The fifth attitude basic to Christian prayer, Jesus tells us, is the desire to live a good and godly life. It is the admission of our humanity, our limitations and an awareness of the natural weaknesses. It reminds us who we really are.

Such simplicity in prayer cements the relationship between the soul that knows itself and the creator-God who knows it, too. It is always and only a matter of bringing the heart back again and again to God's call to honor, commitment, trust, forgiveness, and dedication to the good.

**MANTRA:** *Give me, great God, the simplicity it takes to put myself before you with all my needs knowing without doubt that the one who made me will complete me, as well.*

Abba God in heaven, hallowed be your name! May your reign come; may your will be done on earth as it is in heaven; give us today the bread of Tomorrow. And forgive us our debts, as we hereby forgive those who are indebted to us. Don't put us to the test, but free us from evil. ❧ MATTHEW 6:9–13

# 35. Openheartedness

*When we pray to God we must be seeking
nothing—nothing.*

         ❧ ST. FRANCIS OF ASSISI

The truly prayerful person, the person adult in the ways of the Spirit, does not pray to get things. The person of mature faith prays only to become like the One who leads us to the fullness of God. We pray to become more like Jesus, always more and more immersed in God as time goes by.

A young monastic went on a long and arduous journey into the desert to see a holy one of great repute. "Why did you go all that way?" friends asked him when he returned. "Did you go to ask the Holy One a question?"

"No," said the young disciple. "I did not ask questions."

"Did you go to beg for a spiritual favor?"

"No," said the young disciple. "I did not beg for favors."

"Then why did you go?" the friends persisted.

"I went to watch him sip his soup," the young monastic replied.

Prayer is like that. We go simply to come to know God in every small way we can here so that we ourselves can become more like the God we seek.

To bring ourselves to sense the God-life within us, to sit in silence and allow the soul to be nourished under the impulse of the Spirit is to grow in wisdom and age and grace. It lifts us above the tumult of the world around us. It deepens our understanding of what it is to live in the sight of God. It brings us closer to seeing God face to face, heart to heart, mind to mind.

We do not go to prayer to coax God to create the world according to our personal designs and fancies. We are there to learn how to live well in the life and world we have.

A life of prayer is not an exercise in spiritual athleticism. We do not go down into prayer every day just to prove to ourselves that we can do it. We go down into prayer in order to become both more humble before the God who made us and more confident that the God who made us will sustain us in our limitations. We go down into prayer to become like the One whose life lives in us.

**MANTRA:** *God, show me yourself so that I myself might become more like you. Free me from whatever it is in me that stands between us.*

Six days before Passover, Jesus went to Bethany, the village of Lazarus, whom Jesus had raised from the dead. There they gave a banquet in Jesus' honor, at which Martha served. Lazarus was one of those at the table. Mary brought a pound of costly ointment, pure nard, and anointed the feet of Jesus, wiping them with her hair. The house was full of the scent of the ointment.  JOHN 12:1–3

# 36. Universalism

*We must move from asking God to take care of the things that are breaking our hearts to praying about the things that are breaking God's heart.*

— MARGARET GIBB

The person who learns to pray with the heart of God has no patience for injustice anywhere. They see with the prophet's eye. They break down national boundaries. They transcend gender roles. They have no sense of color or caste, of wealthy or poor. They see only humanity in all its glory, all its pain.

The person of prayer is not a person of private agendas. The more we become like God, the greater-hearted we become as well. We have no sense anymore of "we and they" or "them and us" or "me and mine." Now our hearts open to take in the heart of the world.

"I have heard the cry of my people in Egypt," God says to Moses in the Book of Exodus. "And I intend to deliver them. So, I am sending you to pharaoh to say 'Let my people go.'" The words are the foundation of the prayer bond between us.

When, in prayer, we come to discover God's universal love we suddenly realize that God does not take sides, that we have no priority on God alone. We finally understand that the God we seek is the God of the world and so, to seek that God, we must develop hearts as big as the world ourselves.

Then, racism makes no sense and sexism is as much a sin as any other kind of discrimination, and war is blasphemy against humanity. Then we become bigger than our single nation, broader than any one religion, truly catholic—universal—in our cares and beliefs and commitments.

To develop a cosmic heart is a moment of profound transformation. We can never be the same again. We are beyond the boundaries we have created to separate the human race into my race and theirs.

Then prayer becomes truly co-creative.

Otherwise prayer is nothing more than some kind of spiritual spa designed to make me feel good. It is reduced to an exercise the intent of which is to assure me of my own value. It swaddles me in self-righteousness and self-serving. It makes God an icon, a tribal God whose concerns are no bigger than our own. Then God carries a flag, becomes a male potentate, excludes females, and passes out personal gifts.

Then we make ourselves God and our God a poor, miserable creature indeed—a national patriot, maybe; a great male warrior, perhaps, but certainly not the God of all creation. Then we are simply worshipping ourselves and calling it prayer.

**MANTRA:** *Give me a heart as broad as your own so that I might see You in everyone, everywhere and respond with love and service.*

God said to Cain, "Where is Abel your brother?" Cain answered, "I don't know. Am I my brother's keeper?" God said to Cain, "What have you done? Listen! I hear Abel's blood crying to me from the earth!"   ❧ GENESIS 4:9–10

# 37. Trust

*An old rabbi crossed the village square each morning on his way to the temple to pray. One morning a Cossack accosted him saying, "Hey, Rabbi, where are you going?"*

*And the old rabbi said, "I don't know."*

*The Cossack was furious. "Don't get smart with me," he bellowed. "Every morning for twenty-five years you have crossed this square to go to the temple to pray! You know very well where you're going!"*

*Then the Cossack grabbed the old man by his coat and dragged him off to jail. Just as he was about to throw him into a cell, the rabbi turned to him saying, "See what I mean, I don't know."*

❧ JOSEPH GOLDSTEIN

It's when we begin to take life for granted that we most need to learn to pray.

The truth is that all the while we are making plans for what we will do next and how we will go about doing it, life happens. The stock market falls, the job disappears, the plane doesn't leave on time, the project fails. Everything we mapped out for our lives, for our future, for the moment, simply goes awry.

Then, the God-problem raises its ugly head. Why did God do this to me? What did I do to deserve this? Why doesn't God fix it? How is it that God ignores our prayer? As George Bernard Shaw writes, "Most people do not pray; they only beg." But somewhere along the line, if we are ever to grow up spiritually, the whole notion that prayer is about learning how to make life what I want it to be, dissolves. Obviously it doesn't work.

Depression sets in. We stop praying completely. We stop going to church. We begin to toy with the notion that the whole prayer thing has been some kind of hoax. Did we say the wrong prayers? Did we overlook some part of the ritual that would certainly have assured our success? Does God not love us?

In these early stages of prayer, prayer itself is the question. Worse: God is the question, too. So what are we missing here?

The purpose of prayer is the process of falling into God. As the mystics say, we are beginning to learn that God alone is enough.

The truth is that none of us really knows where we are going and must never take it for granted that we do. We can plan our lives but we cannot guarantee them.

When our prayers are not answered, we know only one thing for sure: The challenge of life now is to live it differently. And it will be through prayer that we discover how to do that. Seeing Jesus being driven out of town, we come to understand that we cannot expect more. Seeing Jesus depressed in the Garden of Olives, we understand that depression is not the loss of faith, it is the moment of faith. Seeing Jesus lose favor with the authorities, we learn that authorities are not the final measure of our lives.

Then we come to prayer free of the desires that bind us, free to live life in God, free to choose trust over certainty—which really means free to choose God over self.

**MANTRA:** *Give me the trust it takes to go through life confident in your care and your love through all the twists and turns of life.*

Be on your guard lest your spirits become bloated with indulgence, drunkenness and worldly cares. That day will suddenly close in on you like a trap. It will come upon all who dwell on the face of the earth, so be on your watch. Pray constantly for the strength to escape whatever comes, and to stand secure before the Chosen One. ❧ LUKE 21:34–36

# 38. Realism

*Call on God but row away from the
rocks.*    ❧ INDIAN PROVERB

Healthy prayer and neurotic prayer are two
different things.

Neurotic prayer denies reality. Healthy prayer
grows both spiritually and psychologically as a
result of it.

The Russian novelist, Ivan Turgenev, warns us of
the danger of the first: "Whatever a person prays
for," Turgenev writes, "they pray for a miracle. Every
prayer reduces itself to this: 'Great God, grant that
twice two be not four.'"

When we fail to accept the fact some things just
are: that rain rains and sickness comes and the unexpected is a commonplace—when we fail to realize
that life is life, all of it meant to teach us something,

to give us new opportunities to be better, stronger people—we miss both the meaning of life and the real role of prayer in it.

The spiritually mature person does not rely on God for miracles. They rely on God for strength and courage, for insight and hope, for vision and endurance. They know that God is with them; they do not believe that God is an instrument for the comfort of human beings.

They do know that one of the purposes of prayer is to give them the courage it takes to do what we are each meant to do in the world that is ours. They do not forgive themselves the responsibility for changing their own little piece of the world on the grounds that if they pray hard enough God will change the world for them. They know that, without doubt, it is their responsibility to change the world.

The mystic Catherine of Siena, whose relationship with God was legendary, changed her part of the world by chiding popes and feeding the poor.

The mystic Ignatius of Loyola, whose life of prayer is exactly what took him and his men to the streets of Europe, changed the world by defending the faith and re-catechizing a generation gone dry.

The contemplative Thomas Merton, whose life in a

cloistered religious community made prayer the context of his very life, changed the world by speaking out from the cloister to lead an anti-war movement intent on stopping the illegal war in Vietnam.

The laywoman Dorothy Day, whose life of prayer followed a tumultuous life, changed the world by modeling the care of the poor on the streets of New York City.

None of the great spiritual personalities of the Church have ever made prayer a substitute for justice and mercy, for peace and equality, for honesty and courage.

They "rowed the world away from the rocks," made the miracles the world needed—and so must we.

**MANTRA:** *Give me, Loving God, the understanding that the purpose of prayer is to grow a soul large enough to do your will.*

But with assistance from Jesus, the child stood up. When Jesus arrived at the house, the disciples asked him privately, "Why is it that we could not expel it?" Jesus replied, "This kind can't be driven out at all—except through prayer." — MARK 9:27–29

# 39. Consistency

*"What action shall I perform to attain God?" the seeker asked.*

*"To attain God," the elder replied, "there are two things you must know. The first is that all efforts to attain God are of no avail."*

*"And the second?" the seeker asked.*

*"You must act as if you did not know the first," the elder said.*

❧ ANTHONY D MELLO, SJ

Prayer is a cultivated state of life. It takes time. It takes attention. Most of all, it takes consistency.

Consistency is what raises simple regularity to the level of relationship. It is possible to pray for hours every day—alone or in a group—and in the end have developed very little depth of soul in the process. Consistency means that I come back to consciousness of God day after day, hour after hour, all my life, whether it is a scheduled event or not. It is the awareness of God that draws me, whether or not I feel any immediate personal satisfaction in doing so or not. I reach out to God whether I can sense God reaching back or not.

All relationships take nourishing—this one with God more than most. So many things draw us away from it. We live on the plane of the tangible and feed it with things and events and people. Those are the things that occupy our minds. The spiritual plane we take for granted though nothing affects us more than the loss of it.

When we're lonely or depressed or agitated or frightened, the material is of little or no help at all. Then, the things we own or collect may actually be part of our problem. What we really need then is the anchoring that only the spiritual can bring. We need the awareness that though life is not in our hands right now, it is surely in the hands of a God who loves us.

It is this anchoring in the spiritual that lifts us above the pressures of the present to the renewed consciousness of the eternal stability of the God who "wishes our well and not our woe."

Without consistency of consciousness, we stand to give ourselves over to the immediate and ephemeral, to the temporary and the meaningless. We lose our balance. We lose our sense of our own nature, let alone the nature of God. We lose our way.

Then the light goes out of life and darkness becomes the state of mind, the color of the future, the cast of the present.

It is consistency of consciousness, the effort to put ourselves in the presence of God over and over again in the course of the day, that prepares us for the abiding Presence that is the home of the soul.

When we give up the practice of the presence of God, it is not God who withdraws from us. It is we who have withdrawn from God. We have taken our heart and given it to what will surely break it eventually. We have taken our mind and centered it on shifting sands. We have given ourselves like falling leaves off a tree in autumn to what cannot and will not last.

"Only in God," the poet says, "is my heart at rest."

In the long run, then, it is consistency, the everlasting turning toward God, that prepares the way for the eternal presence of God in the here and now.

**MANTRA:** *In the morning my soul longs for you, O God. All the day long, I cry for you.*

Come to me, all you who labor and carry heavy burdens, and I will give you rest. Take my yoke upon your shoulders and learn from me, for I am gentle and humble of heart. Here you will find rest for your souls, for my yoke is easy and my burden is light. ❧ MATTHEW 11:28–30

# 40. Integrity

*The Spirit once led the saintly Antony
of the desert to the home of a physician
where he told Antony he would show him
his equal. Antony asked the physician,
"What do you do?" And the physician
replied, "I heal those who come to me.
More than I need I do not take. More
than I can use, I give to the poor, and all
day I sing the Sanctus in my heart."*

🍂 *TALES OF THE DESERT FATHERS AND MOTHERS*

There may be only one thing worse than failing
to value prayer as the link between God and
me here in preparation for an eternal link to come
and that may be in treating prayer as an end in itself.
That may be the assumption that developing a life of
prayer is enough to make me a spiritual person.

Disregard for the spiritual dimension of life is a sure sign of shallow self-sufficiency, of course. In a technological world, the temptation to assume that I am my own God is a common one.

But treating prayer as a talisman, a magic potion, an end in itself is the other side of the problem. It is possible to affect being a spiritual person, even to myself, simply by making a god out of prayer itself.

Only when the life I live mirrors the prayers I say is there any real integrity to the life I'm living.

If we thank God for the good that comes to us but do nothing to bring that same good to others, what is the use of the prayer? If we believe that a spiritual life is the rudder by which we steer our way through life but show no signs of the relationship between what I pray and what I do, what is the use of it all?

I am not here to preen on being spiritual. I am here to develop the spiritual life that makes me a spiritual presence in the life of the world. Anything else, even prayer, is self-gratification not spiritual growth.

**MANTRA:** *Give me a heart, O God, that lives for you. Then, give me commitment to the work that makes that possible.*

Why do you call out, "Rabbi, Rabbi," but don't put into practice what I teach you? Those who come to me and hear my words and put them into practice—I'll show you who they're like: they are like the person who, in building a house, dug deeply and laid the foundation on a rock. When the flood arose, the torrent rushed against the house, but failed to shake it because of its solid foundation.   🌿 LUKE 6:46–48

# 41. Enlightenment

*Meditation, then, is bringing the mind home.* ❧ SOGYAL RINPOCHE

"Always remember, dear sisters," the novice mistress repeated over and over to the young seekers she trained, "the empty vessel must be filled. Otherwise, you have nothing to give to anyone else."

The question is, with what are we to be filled if our prayer life is to be rich and real, deep and developmental? There comes a time in every relationship—including our relationship with God—when chatter is not enough. To sustain the power of an acquaintanceship, it becomes important to come to know the other person—every part of them. Every thought they've ever had. Everything they've ever done. Every ideal they hold. Every hope they nourish.

A real relationship deepens with time until words are not necessary and silence is no burden.

Meditation is the stage between words and silence in the spiritual life. The prayer of words instructs us in the tradition of belief we hold. It teaches us the ideas of the ancients and the prayer forms of the community. Silence takes us beyond words to total consciousness of the Presence that is more than time and greater than life. Meditation fills us with the details of the search.

Meditation milks the sacred Scriptures of every ounce of meaning and history the tradition enshrines for us. It fills us with the great moments of the faith and the great mysteries of the faith, as well. It gives us the framework it takes to meld my life with the life of the one I follow.

Then, the seeking of God, the growth to wholeness, is not a product of folly and fantasy. It is a history of what it means to take this path. It is the definition of what we seek. It is a call to choose between the empty self and the emptying of the self into a spiritual life that makes life meaningful and us whole.

**MANTRA:** *Great God, come to me in silence; turn to mist the words that separate me from you—me from myself.*

Rising early the next morning, Jesus went off to a lonely place in the desert and prayed there.  *❧ MARK 1:35*

# 42. Attention

*Absolute attention is prayer.*

❧ SIMONE WEIL

Prayer should be short and pure, unless it is prolonged under the inspiration of divine grace (*Rule of Benedict*, Chapter 20).

Prayer is the breath of the soul, the life-energy of the spirit. It is the story of the interplay between God and me. It is the link between the inner and the outer life. It has its own rhythm. It is its own reality. There is no formula for it beyond the need to nourish it with both words and silence. But the process is a clear one, nevertheless.

Prayer is made up of two dimensions. In the first, we breathe in the tradition, the faith, the search for God that has nurtured the spiritual life in others down through the ages. In the second, we breathe out the consciousness, the presence, the magnetism of the God who resides in our own heart, uniquely and privately ours.

Benedict of Nursia, in his classic sixth-century rule for monastics, after writing twelve chapters on the ordering of the psalms in seven distinct daily prayer periods for his communities, ends the work with what might easily be read as a shocking, even contradictory, pronouncement. He says clearly and succinctly, "Prayer should be short and pure." How do we explain the tension between the two positions?

Once we understand the purpose and role of words in the spiritual life, the meaning is obvious. The prayer of words is simply meant to fill our minds and thoughts with an awareness of the nature of God and the attitudes of soul needed to immerse ourselves in the God-life.

Then, once that is accomplished, as the philosopher Simone Weil states tersely, prayer becomes "absolute attention." We melt into the presence of God within. There the Great Silence of God becomes the central, major focus of our lives, the anchor of our hearts, the stabilizer that carries us through all the moments of life—with all the emotional upheavals that implies—on a straight and steady course directly to the heart of God.

It captures all our attention. It becomes Liberator, Guide, and Center of our lives until the moment when, all of life's beauty and sorrow over, we melt into the life of God, complete in our growing, certain of our journey, drawn like a moth to a flame.

All the words of faith have prepared us; all the attention to the Silence has burned away the dross. We are ready now. We are finally whole.

**MANTRA:** *Loving God, be in me so that I may be the sign of your presence to many.*

Rejoice always, pray constantly, and give thanks for everything.    ✣ I THESSALONIANS 5:16